ROCK CLIMBING

FOR FUN!

By Dana Meachen Rau

Content Adviser: Bob Culp, American Mountain Guides Association, Certified Guide, Boulder, Colorado
Reading Adviser: Frances J. Bonacci, Ed.D., Reading Specialist, Cambridge, Massachusetts

Compass Point Books ✦ Minneapolis, Minnesota

Compass Point Books
3109 West 50th Street, #115
Minneapolis, MN 55410

Photographs ©: Greg Epperson/Jupiter Images, cover (left); Vasiliy Ganzha/Shutterstock, cover (right), back cover; Jupiter Images, 4 (left); Tyler Olson/Shutterstock,
4–5, 9; Stephen Meese/Shutterstock, 6; Alysta/Shutterstock, 7; Robcocquyt/Shutterstock, 11 (left); Bruno Medley/123RF, 11 (right); Juriah Mosin/Shutterstock, 12–13;
BananaStock/Jupiter Images, 13 (right); Midkhat Izmaylov/Fotolia, 14; ImageShop/Jupiter Images, 15 (top); Philippe Dubocq/Fotolia, 15 (bottom); Goran Kuzmanovski/
Shutterstock, 16; Marion Wear/123RF, 17 (top); Image Source/Jupiter Images, 17 (bottom); Steve Estvanik/123RF, 18–19; Eric Limon/BigStockPhoto, 19 (right); Ben De
Loup/Fotolia, 21; Michel Bordieu/Fotolia, 22 (top); Bob Winsett/Jupiter Images, 22 (bottom); Hemera Technologies/Jupiter Images, 23; Ingram Publishing/Jupiter Images,
24–25; Matt Theilen/Fotolia, 25 (bottom); Eric Limon/Shutterstock, 27 (top); Juha-Pekka Kervinen/Shutterstock, 27 (bottom); Paul Williams/Shutterstock, 29 (left); David
McLain/Aurora/Getty Images, 29 (right); Carsten Medom Madsen/Shutterstock, 30–31; Galyna Andrushko/Shutterstock, 31 (right); Geir Olav Lyngfjell/Shutterstock,
32–33, 47; Shutterstock, 33 (right); Julien Rousset/Fotolia, 34; Robert Fullerton/Shutterstock, 35; Nicholas K. Lim/Shutterstock, 36–37; Jörg Jahn/Shutterstock, 37 (right);
AP Images/Keystone/Olivier Maire, 38; Jose Azel/Aurora/Getty Images, 39; Dana Meachen Rau, 40, 41; Time Life Pictures/Mansell/Getty Images, 42 (left); Roger Viollet
Collection/Getty Images, 42 (right); AP Images, 43; Pavol Kmeto/123RF, 44 (top); Charles Taylor/123RF, 44 (bottom); Andi Berger/Dreamstime, 45.

Editor: Brenda Haugen
Page Production: Ashlee Schultz
Photo Researcher: Eric Gohl
Creative Director: Keith Griffin
Editorial Director: Nick Healy
Managing Editor: Catherine Neitge

Special thanks to Jackie Martin for sharing her
rock-climbing knowledge and experiences for this book.

Library of Congress Cataloging-in-Publication Data
Rau, Dana Meachen, 1971—
  Rock climbing for fun! / by Dana Meachen Rau ; content adviser, Bob Culp ; reading adviser, Frances J. Bonacci.
    p. cm. — (For fun)
  Includes index.
  ISBN 978-0-7565-3396-0 (library binding)
1. Rock climbing—Juvenile literature. I. Title. II. Series.
  GV200.2.R38 2008
  796.522'3—dc22   2007032690

Visit Compass Point Books on the Internet at www.compasspointbooks.com
or e-mail your request to custserv@compasspointbooks.com

Table of Contents

The Basics

Doing It

People, Places, and Fun

Note: In this book, there are two kinds of vocabulary words. Rock-Climbing Words to Know are words specific to rock climbing. They are defined on page 46. Other Words to Know are helpful words that are not related only to rock climbing. They are defined on page 47.

From the Bottom to the Top

Ahhh! The fresh outdoor air makes a hike a great way to spend the day. You may spot a huge rock up ahead. Do you feel the urge to run over and see how fast you can scurry to the top?

If so, rock climbing may be for you. Rock climbing is the sport of ascending a steep rock surface. It is up to you to get from the bottom to the top, even though you climb with a group. People of all ages enjoy rock climbing, so it is a fun sport to enjoy with your family and friends.

What do you need to make that climb? You need strong arms and legs. You need a partner whom you trust. You need gear to keep you safe. You need to be patient and willing to take your time to find the best route up. You also need a sense of adventure. It will not be easy to reach the top. But when you do, the view and the whole experience will make it worthwhile.

The most important part of climbing is to be safe. Never try climbing on your own. Always have an adult watching you.

Don't Give Up

The more you climb, the better you will get. Sometimes taking a chance will help you become a better climber.

But it is OK to stop, too. You do not need to do anything that makes you feel unsafe. The most important thing is that you tried.

The Highest and the Hardest

Mont Blanc

From the beginning of history, people saw summits covered with rocks, snow, or clouds. Some of them started to venture up these mountains to see what they were like at the top.

But it is the 1786 ascent of Mont Blanc, the highest mountain of the Alps, that is often considered the beginning of rock climbing. Soon people started to explore other mountain ranges around the world.

Special climbing ropes and other gear were introduced in the early 1900s. As the century went on and more people wanted to climb, equipment improved. With better equipment, people started conquering climbs that they hadn't been able to do before. The summit of Mount Everest, the highest mountain in the world, was finally reached in 1953.

Ascending mountains is called mountaineering, which combines hiking, rock climbing, and ice climbing. To train for mountaineering, people climbed shorter faces of rock. In the 1950s, rock climbing became its own sport.

As more people enjoyed climbing, indoor climbing walls opened. Today people enjoy climbing at their gyms and recreation centers or outdoors all around the world.

With Ropes and Without

Bouldering is climbing on rocks that are not very high, often no more than 10 feet (3 meters). You don't need ropes or a harness, but you do need to follow the rules of safety. Always have an adult watch you. You can also place a bouldering mat below you to land on in case you fall.

Even though the rocks aren't high, bouldering can be a challenge. When people boulder, they focus on tough moves. Their goal is not always to get to the top of the rock. Their goal is often to find ways to traverse, or move across, the rock's surface.

Unlike bouldering, free climbing is climbing from the bottom of the rock to the top. While free climbing, people wear special gear. This equipment is not there to help you get up the rock, however. It is only there to help you if you fall.

Top-roping is the safest way to free climb. One end of the rope is attached to the climber. Then the rope goes through an anchor at the top. The other end is attached to a belayer, a person who is there to stop the climber if he or she falls.

From Pitch to Pitch

Experts may do several types of free climbing. In traditional climbing, or trad climbing, a climber and belayer work together and are attached to each other by a rope. The lead climber climbs up the rock face a bit and wedges an anchor into a crack in the rock. The more he pulls on the anchor, the more secure it gets.

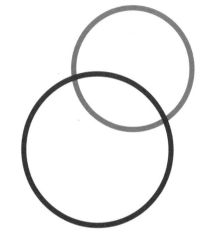

The climber then ties his rope to the anchor. As he keeps ascending the rock, he puts in more anchors. The belayer is holding on to the rope tightly at the bottom, so if the climber falls, he will only fall as far as the last anchor.

When the climber goes as far as the rope allows, called a pitch, it is the belayer's turn to climb. From a safe stopping point, the first climber now becomes the belayer and helps his partner ascend. The new climber removes the anchors as he climbs up the rock.

This is a difficult type of climbing and only for experts. There are moments when the lead climber is on the rock without anything holding him there.

In sport climbing, there are permanent anchors in the rock. This is much safer than trad climbing, but the climbers don't get to choose their own routes.

No Matter What the Weather

What if it's raining and you are in a climbing mood? Or what if it's the middle of winter and you don't want to climb outside in the cold and snow? Then you can climb indoors!

Indoor climbing has become a popular sport. Many gyms have climbing walls. These walls are made of wood or concrete. They have plastic handholds and footholds bolted into them. Handholds and footholds come in many shapes, just like the many types of natural handholds and footholds you would find on a rock face outdoors.

Indoor gyms are a good choice in areas that don't have many outdoor places to climb. And they offer climbing no matter what the weather or season. Some experts even train on indoor walls to work on new moves.

In a gym, you will use the top-roping technique. In fact, one of the safest and best ways to start climbing is to take lessons at a gym with a climbing wall.

Easy to See

Handholds and footholds on indoor climbing walls are made of plastic. They come in many shapes and sizes and are often brightly colored. That way a climber can easily see them on the wall.

The Gear You Need

You need a lot of gear to climb. When you take a climbing class, the instructor will provide the gear for you. If you want to do a lot more climbing, you will have to buy your own.

Rope: A kermantle rope, or climbing rope, is made especially for rock climbing. It has a strong braided nylon center called the *kern*. The kern is surrounded by a braided nylon covering called the *mantle*. This double layer makes the rope strong. If the outer layer gets a little worn, the inside is still protected. Climbing ropes are usually about 165 feet (50 m) long, and they come in colorful patterns.

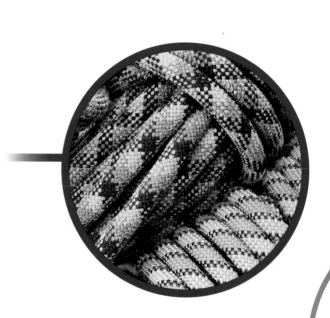

Harness: Both the climber and belayer wear harnesses. You step into the harness's leg holes and then secure the harness around your waist. The harness has a loop in the front, where you attach yourself to the rope. Some harnesses have other loops to carry gear.

Helmet: A climbing helmet is hard on the outside. The inside is padded to make it comfortable. You need to make sure your helmet is on correctly. It should sit on top of your head and cover your forehead. You click it closed under your chin and then adjust the chin strap so that it is snug.

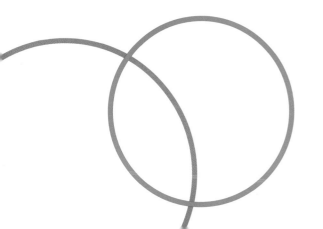

Dynamics

A climbing rope is dynamic. That means it will stretch a little. A stretchy rope is gentler when you fall, since you don't stop so suddenly.

Even More Gear You Need!

Carabiners (Biners): Biners are pear-shaped aluminum loops that climbers use to attach the rope to anchors or to the belayer and the climber. For climbing, you need to be sure to use the type that locks. Biners have a gate, or opening, where you can slip the rope through. The gate locks either by screwing it closed or with a special spring that keeps it shut.

Belay device: The belayer clips the belay device to his harness with a carabiner. The rope passes smoothly through the belay device as the climber is ascending. Some belay devices pinch the rope, helping it to stop.

Shoes: Climbing shoes have rubber bottoms that stick to small footholds and help you "feel" the rock through your shoes. If you get climbing shoes, they should fit tightly, and your feet should not slip around inside them. For beginning climbers, a good pair of sneakers will work.

Chalk: Some climbers hook a bag filled with chalk powder to their waists when they climb. They rub the chalk on their hands to keep them dry. The chalk absorbs their sweat and helps climbers get a better grip on the rock.

What to Wear

When climbing, you should wear comfortable clothing, such as a T-shirt and shorts or long, soft pants. If your clothes are too loose, they can keep your harness from fitting correctly. Also be careful of zippers, buttons, or buckles that lie under the harness. They might rub against your skin.

Check and Double-check

You can get hurt doing almost any sport. You could get hit by a baseball. You could trip while you run. But with rock climbing, there are more serious dangers. If you fall off a rock, you could get severely hurt. So you have to be sure to be as safe as you can when you rock climb.

Take a rock climbing lesson first. You will learn about all the equipment. You will learn how to best find handholds and footholds. You will learn how to be safe.

Always wear a helmet. You need to protect your head from falling objects—such as rocks or gear—from the rock face, and from the ground if you fall.

Make sure your harness is on correctly and is snug but comfortable. The front loop should be at your belly button. After you adjust the straps, double back the straps into the buckles.

Always check all carabiners to make sure they are locked and that all knots are tight. Check your rope before and after every climb to make sure that it is not frayed. Never step on the rope. Most important, only go rock climbing with an experienced adult climber!

Low but Tough

That's a big rock in front of you. How will you begin bouldering? Just climb on and give it a try. Climbing uses muscles in your arms and legs. But it is best to do most of the work with your legs, and use your arms and hands more for balance.

As you find each foothold, push down on it with your legs and step up. It will not be like climbing a ladder. You will need to balance on tiny pieces of rock. You step up with one foot, and then reach up for a handhold with the opposite hand. Then step up with your other foot, and reach up with the opposite hand. Before you know it, you will be climbing up—that is, if you can find handholds and footholds!

Gear

- Helmet
- Climbing shoes (or sneakers)
- Chalk and chalk bag (optional)
- Bouldering pad (soft foam mat)

If you can't find handholds or footholds, you might have to traverse the rock. That means moving sideways instead of up.

If you just can't find anywhere else on the rock to go, you can climb down. If you have to, you can jump. But bend your knees when you land so you don't hurt your legs.

The fact that bouldering is done near the ground does not mean you should do it alone. A more experienced climber should be your spotter. A spotter is someone ready to help you if you slip off the rock.

Working Together

When top-roping, an experienced climber will first set up the anchor at the top of the climb. The anchor can be natural, such as a strong tree or a rock. Or it can be gear that someone put in, such as bolts permanently drilled into the rock. The anchor has to be solid and strong. The climber will attach a carabiner to the anchor or use a top-rope device and pass the rope through.

Next the climber needs to tie in. That means connecting the carabiner on your harness to the climbing rope. An experienced climber might use a figure-eight follow-through or a double figure-eight knot to do this. These knots get tighter as you pull

on them. The belayer will slip the other end of the rope through his or her belay device, which is attached to the belay loop on the harness.

When everyone is tied in, and all biners, knots, and harnesses are checked, you are ready to begin. The climber and belayer use certain commands to communicate with each other. A belayer's job is to keep the climber safe at all times. As the climber ascends, the belayer pulls down on the rope and takes in the slack created by the rope. That way, if the climber falls, the belayer can stop the rope, and the climber will not fall far.

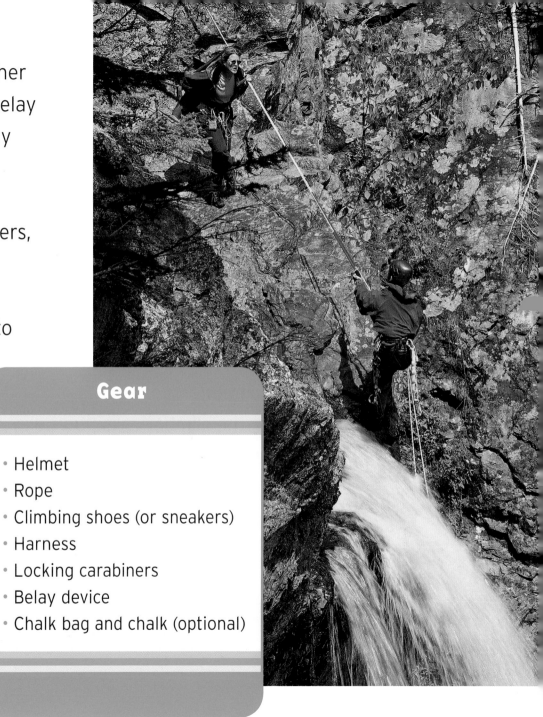

Gear

- Helmet
- Rope
- Climbing shoes (or sneakers)
- Harness
- Locking carabiners
- Belay device
- Chalk bag and chalk (optional)

Climbing Calls

The climber and belayer need to talk to each other during the climb, so a system of calls has been created for them to use.

To start a climb:

When ready, the climber asks "On belay?"
If ready, the belayer responds "Belay on."

When starting to ascend, the climber says "Climbing."
The belayer says "Climb" to let the climber know he has started to belay.

During the climb:

If the climber needs the belayer to let out more rope, he says "Slack."

If the climber wants the belayer to take in more rope, he says "Take in" or "Up rope."

A falling climber yells "Falling!" to let the belayer know to hold on.

After the climb:

When safe on top and ready to be released from the belayer, the climber says "Belay off."

The belayer says "Off belay" to let the climber know that he has stopped belaying.

Look Out Below!

If a rock is falling, the climber yells "Rock!" to warn others below.

If a climber at the top is tossing down a rope to his partner, he yells "Rope!"

Get a Grip!

Sometimes a rock face looks smooth, and you can't see any good places to grab. Sometimes a rock is full of bumps and cracks, which are perfect for you to hold with your hands. You will be amazed at how you can hold yourself up and keep your balance while using your hands and feet on small surfaces.

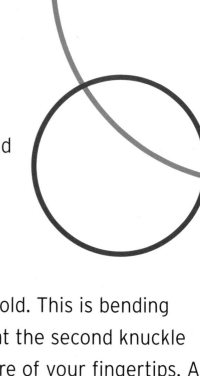

Climbers use various hand grips to hold on to a rock. One method is the open grip. This is great for nice large handholds, called jugs or buckets. You just grab the hold with your whole hand and pull yourself up. On smaller handholds, you might use a crimp hold. This is bending your fingers at the second knuckle and using more of your fingertips. A pinch grip is using your thumb and fingers like a claw. For cracks, you can jam your hand in to hold on to the wall.

Strong Hands

To strengthen your fingers, you can do some exercises. Wrap a rubber band around your four fingertips and thumb so it is tight. Spread your fingers, and then relax them. You can also squeeze a tennis ball.

Stepping Up!

Now that you know how to grip the rock with your hands, you'll have to find places to put your feet. You may be amazed, but sometimes your feet can fit onto a nub, or small piece of rock, that is even too small to use as a handhold.

If you can't put your foot flat on a foothold, edging is one method to try. You use the edge of your shoe, at the toe, heel, or even the side, to step onto a foothold. If there is just no foothold at all, and you have climbing shoes, you can use smearing. This means rubbing your foot as flat onto the rock as you can, so that most of the sole is in contact with the rock. Your shoe might be just sticky enough to hold you on.

Your legs are your strongest body parts in climbing, so use them! You may feel you need to grab on with your hands and pull up. But it is better to use your legs and push up when you can. It is best to be touching the rock with three

Up the Chimney

To climb up a chimney, which is a name for a big crack, you'll need more than just your hands and feet. Wedge your whole body into the crack, and lean on one side with your back. With your hands and feet on the opposite side, you can slowly shimmy up the wall.

parts—two hands and a foot, or two feet and a hand—at all times. It is also good to be vertical, with your body close to the rock face.

29

What's Your Class?

Climbers have developed a rating system so that they can know how hard a climb is going to be. In the United States, the rating system is called the Yosemite Decimal System (YDS).

There are six classes of climbs:

Class 1: walking on flat ground, such as a sidewalk, bike path, or clear wide trail

Class 2: hiking on an uneven trail

Class 3: scrambling on rocks that are steep enough that you may have to use your hands, but not rope

Class 4: climbing that is hard to do without some safety from a rope

Class 5: rock climbing (the type discussed in this book) that needs gear for safety

Class 6: climbs requiring ladders and other equipment

The YDS rates climbs with two numbers. The first number is the class, and the second tells how hard it is.

5.0 to 5.4–beginner climbs
5.5 to 5.7–intermediate climbs
5.8 to 5.10–expert climbs
5.11 to 5.14–only left to the experts

What a View!

Congratulations! You reached the top of the climb. You may be exhausted. You may have a few scrapes. Your hands and wrists might hurt. But reaching the top of a climb is an exciting moment.

A climb takes patience and the ability to solve problems. You have shown you have both of these things!

When you reach the top, take a moment to look down to see how far you have come. Then take a moment to look around you. Enjoy the fresh air and the chance to rest. You deserve it!

Getting Down

At the top you might get off belay and hike down to your partner if there is a walking trail. If not, the belayer can lower you.

To do this, you lean back on your harness and hold the climbing rope in front of you. The belayer slowly gives you more slack as you "walk" backward down the wall. It is best to stay horizontal so that you have more control.

Instead of being lowered, experts might rappel, or descend by sliding down the rope to the bottom of the rock face.

A climber rappels down a cliff.

Leave It to the Experts!

Expert rock climbers find interesting ways to challenge themselves.

Aid Climbing

In aid climbing, the climbs are so hard or so long that climbers use equipment not just for safety but to help them ascend. Big walls are climbs that take more than one day. People on these climbs have to haul their gear, meals, and water up the rock with them. They also might bring sleeping bags to use on portaledges, which are portable sleeping platforms that they anchor to the rock. Or they might even climb through the night and wear headlights.

Solo Climbing

Solo climbing is the most dangerous type of climbing. It is only for experts with a lot of climbing experience. Solo climbers ascend alone and use no ropes, harnesses, or any type of gear. If they fall, they could die. Some solo climbers ascend cliffs above the sea in hope that the ocean will break their fall.

Ice Climbing

Ice climbing is a lot like rock climbing, but some of the gear is different. Ice climbers use anchors, harnesses, and ropes. But they also use axes to grip the ice and have crampons, or spikes, on their boots. Instead of climbing the sides of mountains, ice climbers ascend frozen waterfalls or glaciers.

Where to Go

The world is full of challenging climbs. El Capitan in Yosemite National Park in California is thought to be the hardest sport climb on the planet. El Capitan is a big-wall climb of more than 3,000 feet (914 m). Its best feature is the Nose, an overhang that is seemingly impossible to ascend. It takes the average climber about five days to ascend the Nose!

Beginners who don't need such big challenges can find many places to climb. If you don't live near any good outdoor climbs, you can probably find a gym or recreation center with an indoor wall.

El Capitan

The Seven Summits

The Seven Summits are the highest mountains of the seven continents.

- **Asia:** Everest, 29,035 feet (8,850 m)
- **South America:** Aconcagua, 22,841 feet (6,962 m)
- **North America:** Denali (Mount McKinley), 20,320 feet (6,194 m)
- **Africa:** Kilimanjaro, 19,341 feet (5,895 m)
- **Europe:** Elbrus, 18,510 feet (5,642 m)
- **Antarctica:** Vinson Massif, 16,066 feet (4,897 m)
- **Australia/Oceania:** Carstensz Pyramid, 16,023 feet (4,884 m)

Keep It Beautiful

Wherever you climb, remember to have respect for the nature around you by leaving the climbing site just as you found it. Climbers should remove all of their anchors, use chalk that is the same color as the rock, and take any trash back home.

Mount Everest

The Best in the World

Some climbers like to compete against others to see who can reach the top the fastest. Or they might compete against themselves and try to beat their previous times on the same climbs.

Competitors race during the speed event at the Ice Climbing World Cup.

Some climbers compete to see who is the best in the world. The first World Cup for climbing was held in 1989. Since then, many international events have been organized. Teams from countries around the world gather to compete in lead climbing, bouldering, and speed climbing.

Climbers ages 14 to 19 compete at the annual World Youth Championships. After a series of qualifying rounds, semifinals, and finals, the judges choose the winner.

Among the Best

Australian Libby Hall is one of the most famous youth climbers. All the training she did every morning before school really paid off. When she was 15, Hall won the gold medal in speed climbing at the 2005 World Youth Championships in Beijing, China.

Lynn Hill has been climbing for more than 30 years and is considered one of the best climbers in the world. In 1994, she free-climbed the Nose of El Capitan in one day. The climb of 33 pitches, or rope lengths, took 23 hours. Through it all Hill kept reminding herself to be patient and relaxed.

Lynn Hill climbs in New York.

On the Tower with Jackie

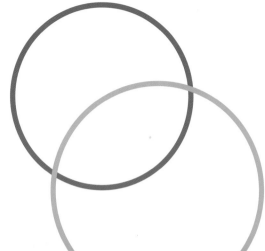

Winding Trails Inc., in Farmington, Connecticut, offers a variety of outdoor adventures. One of the most popular activities is climbing its 40-foot (12-m) outdoor tower. Jackie Martin is an outdoor adventure facilitator there who leads school groups and other classes.

Before class members get on the tower, they play games to get to know one another. They also talk about setting goals for themselves. "Rock climbing is not only about getting to the top," Martin said. "It's also about learning to rock climb and then practicing your skills."

Jackie Martin

Next Martin lets class members know the plan for the day and talks about the equipment. She shows them the tower, which has three sides with handholds and footholds and a fourth side with a huge cargo net.

"My job is to make them feel secure," Martin says. If children are having trouble on the wall, she lets them know it is OK to come down. But she hopes they will be willing to try again.

Getting to the top is exciting. There is a bell for the climber to ring. An even bigger reward is the zip line, which lets the climber glide from the tower into the woods.

At the end of the day, the group gets back together to talk. They have not just learned to climb. "Hopefully these kids can take a piece of their experience back," Martin says, "and learn something about themselves."

What Happened When?

1450	1750	1850	1900	1910	1920	1930

1492 The first recorded aid climb is done by Antoine de Ville of Mont Aiguille in France.

Late 1800s/Early 1900s British, French, and German climbers practice rock-climbing skills on boulders and cliffs to train for mountain climbs.

1786 Dr. Michel Paccard and his guide Jacques Balmat climb to the top of Mont Blanc in France.

Early 1900s The development of specialized climbing equipment, such as carabiners and new types of anchors, helps climbers.

1932 The Union Internationale des Associations d'Alpinisme (UIAA) (International Mountaineering and Climbing Federation) forms to represent rock climbers, ice climbers, and mountaineers.

1850s The first climbing club forms, showing that people take an interest in climbing as a sport.

1940　1950　1960　1970　1980　1990　2000　2010

1960s Shoes with rubber soles made specifically for rock climbing are created.

1953 On May 29, Sir Edmund Hillary of New Zealand and Tenzing Norgay of Nepal are the first to reach the top of Mount Everest, on the border of Nepal and Tibet.

1980s Climbing gyms open.

2007 The ICC becomes the International Federation of Sport Climbing, made up of 48 federations that govern competitive climbing.

1989 The first World Cup for sport climbing is held in Leeds, England.

1999 Bouldering gets its own World Cup.

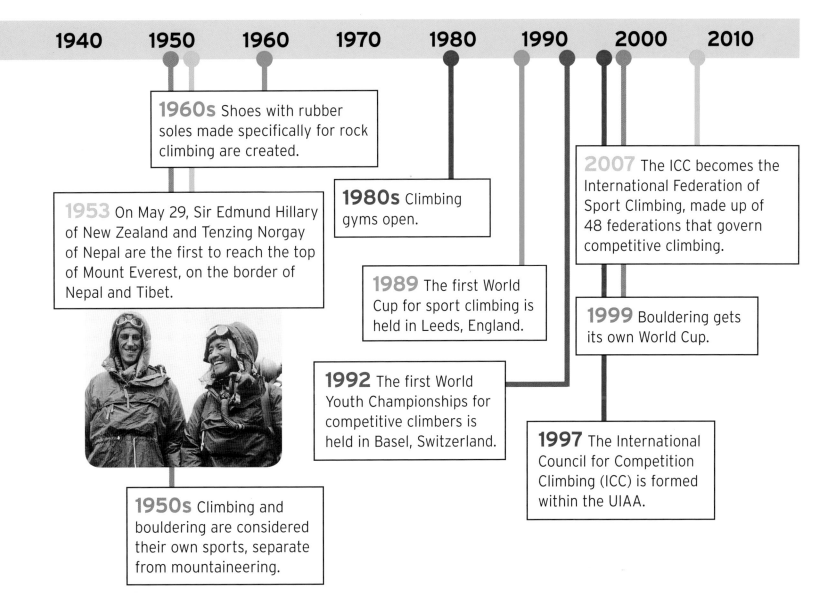

1992 The first World Youth Championships for competitive climbers is held in Basel, Switzerland.

1997 The International Council for Competition Climbing (ICC) is formed within the UIAA.

1950s Climbing and bouldering are considered their own sports, separate from mountaineering.

Fun Rock-Climbing Facts

Alpine climbing is ascending a mountain over a few days, carrying all of your gear with you. That means alpinists try to pack light.

The most popular kinds of rock for climbing are granite, limestone, sandstone, metamorphosed schist, and gneiss.

If the climber weighs much more than the belayer, the belayer can anchor himself or herself to an object. This will keep the belayer from being lifted off the ground as the climber descends.

For a top-rope climb, the distance of the climb has to be less than half the length of the rope. That's because to start, the rope must go from the climber up to the anchor and back down to the belayer.

On the day of competition at the World Youth Championships, climbers enter an isolation zone. They are not allowed to see the climb or talk to people who have seen it. Then they are led out to the wall for a brief period of time so they can make observations and think about the best way to ascend the wall.

Some climbers bring along a high-carbohydrate snack called *gorp*. The letters in gorp stand for "good old raisins and peanuts." You can add many things to this power snack, such as almonds, dried cranberries or other fruit, chocolate chips, or any type of cereal.

Rock-Climbing Words to Know

aid climbing: type of climbing in which a person uses gear to help in the ascent

anchor: gear that connects a person to the rock or a fixed point

belay device: piece of gear that the belayer attaches to his or her harness and threads the rope through

belayer: person holding the other end of a climber's rope to keep the climber from falling

big walls: climbs that take more than a day

bouldering: climbing a rock less than 10 feet (3 m) high

carabiner: aluminum loops used to hook the rope to anchors, or to the climber and the belayer

crampons: spikes on an ice climber's boots

crimp hold: holding by bending your fingers at the second knuckle

edging: using the edges of climbing shoes on a foothold

face: the part of the rock a person is going to climb

free climbing: type of climbing in which a person uses gear for safety, not to help with the ascent

harness: nylon webbing that fits around a person's waist and legs

lead climbing: type of climbing in which a person places anchors while ascending a rock

mountaineering: ascending a mountain using hiking, rock climbing, and ice climbing techniques

open grip: grabbing a handhold with your whole hand

pinch grip: using your thumb and fingers like a claw

pitch: one rope length

portaledge: portable sleeping platform

rappel: descend a rock face by sliding down a rope

slack: loose rope

smearing: rubbing a foot flat onto the rock for a good hold

solo climbing: climbing alone with no safety gear

speed climbing: type of climbing in which one climber races another climber or tries to beat a certain time to the top

sport climbing: type of climbing in which a climber uses anchors that are already placed in the rock

spotter: person below and behind the climber ready to help the climber down so he or she doesn't fall while bouldering

tie in: connecting the harness to the climbing rope

top-roping: climbing with the rope attached to a fixed anchor at the top and held by a belayer

trad climbing: traditional climbing; type of climbing in which a person puts in anchors while ascending

Other Words to Know

ascending: moving upward

dynamic: movable or stretchy

glaciers: large areas of slowly moving ice

horizontal: side to side

recreation: pastimes and hobbies

summits: the tops of mountains

traverse: to move across

vertical: up and down

Where to Learn More

MORE BOOKS TO READ

Crossingham, John, and Bobbie Kalman. *Extreme Sports, No Limits! Extreme Climbing*. New York: Crabtree Publishing Company, 2004.

Venables, Stephen. *To the Top: The Story of Everest*. Cambridge, Mass.: Candlewick Press, 2003.

Weintraub, Aileen. *Rock Climbing*. New York: Children's Press, 2003.

ON THE ROAD

Yosemite National Park
Public Information Office
P.O. Box 577
Yosemite, CA 95389
209/372-0200

Capitol Reef National Park
HC 70 Box 15
Torrey, UT 84775
435/425-3791

ON THE WEB

For more information on this topic, use FactHound.

1. Go to *www.facthound.com*
2. Type in this book ID: 0756533961
3. Click on the *Fetch It* button.

FactHound will find the best Web sites for you.

INDEX

ABOUT THE AUTHOR

Dana Meachen Rau has written more than 200 books for children, both fiction and nonfiction. She loves sitting on her porch to breathe the fresh air, watch for wildlife, and admire the flowers growing in her garden. But her favorite outdoor activity is climbing the outdoor rock wall near her home in Burlington, Connecticut, where she lives with her husband and children. She loves the feeling when she reaches the top.